TRUMPET II

PLAY ALONG WITH THE CANADIAN BRASS

15 INTERMEDIATE PIECES

CANADIAN BRASS

Trumpets: Ryan Anthony, Joe Burgstaller
Horn: Jeff Nelsen
Trombone: Gene Watts
Tuba: Chuck Daellenbach

To access companion recorded performances
and accompaniments* online, visit:
www.halleonard.com/mylibrary

Enter Code
7129-7144-7825-6762

The part remains faintly on the recording for guidance.
Recorded 2001, Toronto; Rob Tremills, engineer

ISBN 978-0-634-04971-2

HAL•LEONARD®

Copyright © 2002 by HAL LEONARD LLC
International Copyright Secured   All Rights Reserved

Visit Hal Leonard Online at
www.halleonard.com
Visit Canadian Brass online at
www.canadianbrass.com

Contact us:
Hal Leonard
7777 West Bluemound Road
Milwaukee, WI 53213
Email: info@halleonard.com

In Europe, contact:
Hal Leonard Europe Limited
42 Wigmore Street
Marylebone, London, W1U 2RN
Email: info@halleonardeurope.com

In Australia, contact:
Hal Leonard Australia Pty. Ltd.
4 Lentara Court
Cheltenham, Victoria, 3192 Australia
Email: info@halleonard.com.au

ANDANTE

from the Trumpet Concerto

Joseph Haydn
(1732-1809)
arranged by Walter Barnes

2nd B♭ CORNET/TRUMPET

PRAYER
from *Hansel and Gretel*

2nd **TRUMPET**

Engelbert Humperdinck
(1854-1921)
arranged by Henry Charles Smith

RONDEAU

Jean-Joseph Mouret
(1682-1738)
arranged by Walter Barnes

2nd B♭ CORNET/TRUMPET

CANON

Johann Pachelbel
(1653-1706)
arranged by Walter Barnes

2nd B♭ CORNET/TRUMPET

WHERE'ER YOU WALK

from *Semele*

George Frideric Handel
(1685-1759)
arranged by Walter Barnes

PILGRIMS' CHORUS

from *Tannhäuser*

Richard Wagner
(1813-1883)
arranged by Henry Charles Smith

2nd TRUMPET

GRAND MARCH
from *Aïda*

Giuseppi Verdi
(1813-1901)
arranged by Walter Barnes

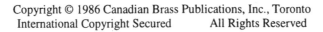

Grand March from Aida *continued*

THREE ELIZABETHAN MADRIGALS

I. My Bonny Lass, She Smileth

Thomas Morely
(1557-1602)
arranged by Walter Barnes

II. Come Again, Sweet Love

John Dowland
(1562-1626)
arranged by Walter Barnes

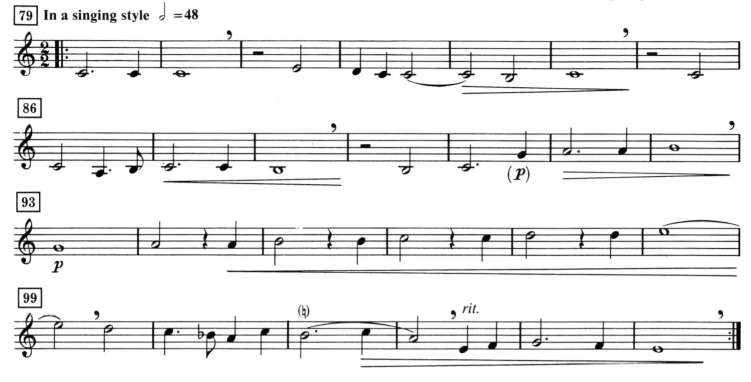

III. Now Is the Month of Maying

Thomas Morely
(1557-1602)
arranged by Walter Barnes

TRUMPET VOLUNTARY

John Stanley
(1713-1786)
arranged by Walter Barnes

Trumpet Voluntary *continued*

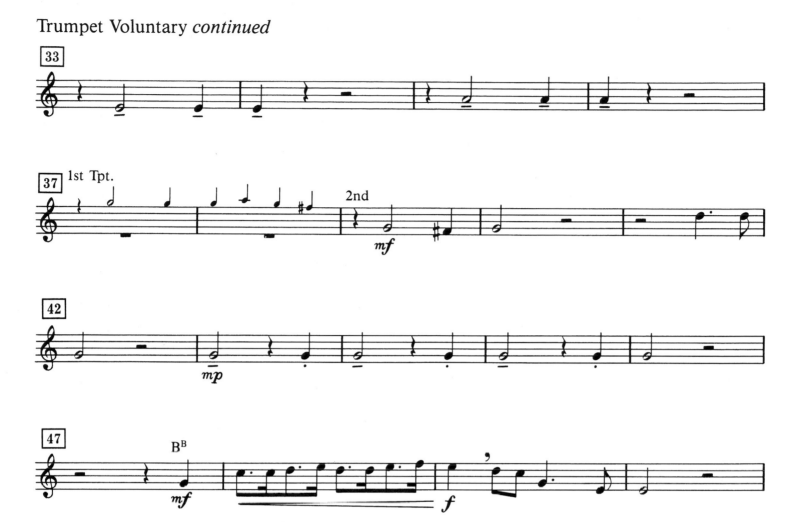

THREE SPIRITUALS

African-American spirituals
arranged by Walter Barnes

Three Spirituals *continued*

AMAZING GRACE

traditional American
arranged by Luther Henderson
adapted by Walter Barnes

2nd B♭ CORNET/TRUMPET